BUSINESS AND SOCIETY TODAY

By

Dr. Efthemia Papadopoulos, Ph.D.

© Happy Everyday

2020

ISBN: 9798694968973

Table of Contents

Acknowledgement 3

Foreword.. 4

Preface... 5

Chapter 1: Introduction to Organizations 6

Chapter 2: Stakeholders 11

Chapter 3: Relationship Management and Ethics............. 13

Chapter 4: Rights and Regulations 19

Chapter 5: Technology... 22

Wrap Up.. 30

Glossary 32

Hyperlink References... 35

BUSINESS AND SOCIETY TODAY

Acknowledgement

Thank you to all who support Happy Everyday and the mission to access enlightenment and love. The leadership and members of Happy Everyday also thank those who have wronged them because in the dark is when having a light is useful.

BUSINESS AND SOCIETY TODAY

Smoking was once promoted by medical doctors and advertised for pregnant women. What are we doing today that 30 years from now will be not smart? Inhaling our mobile devices and forgetting to smell and see the roses.

Foreword

"The world is a scary place, even here, in Numbani, we needed something to protect us. Enter the OR15 defense bots. They took the old Idina (OR14) models from the crisis and gave them a complete makeover. They kept us safe…for a while. I was at the airport when Doomfist attacked. Poor bots…didn't stand a chance. Everyone else gave up on you! But I saw what you could be. So, I rebuilt you! Updated your programming and gave you a <u>heart</u>."

Efi Oladele
Inventor
Orisa Origin <u>Story</u>, Overwatch

"Your safety is my primary concern." ORI5A

BUSINESS AND SOCIETY TODAY

Preface

Welcome. We are here to become aware of the Business, Government, and Society (BGS) field. In this read, government is rolled in to being defined as a business because it is an organization. This material has a safety theme because the safety of citizens and customers is paramount in any society.

Business and Society Today is written as a personal letter to students from me, Dr. P. I use operational definitions to articulate how I have come to view society. The term business can be defined broadly. You will learn about the five types of social interaction and no matter how big or small the interactions, they make up society.

In today's times readers are more receptive of the phrase marriage is business. When I taught sociology in the early 2000's students passionately disagreed but what we are socialized to believe is not business, fundamentally is. We are in a different America today from 20 years ago.

Types of social interactions can be a business for profit; dog walking, ride sharing, healthcare and day care. A group who come together with a particular purpose can make up a family, community, and country. Although a geographic location was described, a business or society is not limited by location.

Safety for citizens, employees, family members, and customers is important, no matter where they are located. A first principle of ethics is safety. Hyperlinks in text are safe.

Chapter 1: Introduction to Organizations

The United States of America has geographic locations on Earth, a government, and stakeholders. Because of American culture, the **organization** that is the USA is also called a society.

There are **macro organizations** and **micro organizations**, businesses, and societies on Earth. The material written here is by a first generation Greek American, born in Danbury, Connecticut, me. Family, interactions, and society made me who I am today. Thank you to John Oliver for the fun about Danbury.

Connecticut is known as the Constitution State, where my **primary socialization** occurred. Music across America was different at the time but video games and sports kids played outside were about the same. Be sure to also look up and read what **secondary socialization** is in the *Glossary*.

A volleyball teammate in high school who relocated to Connecticut (CT) from California (CA) introduced me to music by Sublime. Because **streaming music** was not a thing back then, I listened to <u>freestyle music</u> that gained traction in the 1980's in New York City (NYC) from the radio. Almost everything today has gone **global** or **multinational** because of technology and human enhancement.

Back to macro of USA and micro societies that are the states. The State of California operates differently than Connecticut, as all the states operate differently based on their **state constitutions** and government leadership. But, the states are under a **federal jurisdiction** for some matters, the **federal government** of the United States of America.

<u>California</u> has a culture of its own, as each of the states do too. Heck, even the residents of the north and south of California deem they are different. Having traveled by **electric car** north and south on each coast and east and

west, I have been there and seen that. In the time it takes to charge the battery of an electric car, be it fifteen minutes or an hour, interacting with people in different places and states gives a sense of the micro social sentiment there.

CALIFORNIA REPUBLIC

An American **stakeholder** can be grateful for what they have become accustomed, used to, and familiar with, being primarily and secondarily socialized in America. It is wise to experience a day to day, in person, in another country. The way of life and rules are different between states, let alone differences in living somewhere you are not socialized to live. It is one thing to relocate within the United States and experience life in different states, but how many of you reading this have spent time in other countries?

Can you imagine yourself living and working outside of America? Some of you came to America from other countries. There are some who want to stay and some who want to study here and then return to their home countries and contribute to positive social change there.

BUSINESS AND SOCIETY TODAY

What is your plan?

For me, who spent summers in Greece growing up, but, felt just as excited to get back to school in Connecticut every fall, I knew my career would be to serve America first and then, if I had the resources, energy and impact, serve other societies.

After visiting California and loving the clean air in the nightclubs, because smoking was first banned indoors in California, I fell in love with the progressiveness. In the 1950's, medical doctors were on commercials advertising which cigarette brands to smoke. This goes to show how ignorant we humans are about certain business ventures until they have been around long enough for us to be knowledgeable and aware of what they do to our species.

Technology contributed to making a machine that can mass produce cigarettes so it became a point to manufacture and sell them. Technology enhances humanity at a cost, a cost that humans are willing to, or coerced, to pay. Do you use your mobile device or does your mobile device use you? What we know now about the use of cigarettes is different than what we knew when cigarettes were being marketed and sold for profit. Social media organizations are also for profit.

What will we know 30 years from now about the use of mobile devices on the brain?

Our human species is being rewired by mobile devices and the damages have begun to be seen. How we set our notifications is a matter of health and well being.

Silicon Valley is indeed in California and that is the birth place of the technology giants today. The technology giants are organizations that operate as for profit businesses and typically have their charitable foundation counterparts.

Depending on the type of registered business and corporate governance, based by state, for those in America, and guidelines to operate in other countries, one person or a group of people can have the controlling power. Of course, the status of a company, whether it is publically traded or private, has its permissions and constraints in regards to controlling power. More on controlling power is discussed later with the ethical questions regarding **proxy voting**.

Controlling power within an organization that returns exorbitant profit can yield controlling power in larger organization of societies that a business operates in.

Chapter 2: Stakeholders

In business terms there are market and non-market stakeholders. American citizen or not, you are a stakeholder of the USA, by some level of interest, to read this content or because it is required to pass an exam. After explaining the five types of social interaction, you will know more about stakeholders.

The five types of social interaction are:

1. Cooperation
2. Competition
3. Commerce
4. Conflict
5. Coercion

Review all five types of social interaction and think of how you experience them during the course of your life. Coercion can be challenging but think of being coerced as doing something you really do not want to do but do anyway. Now match the interactions of a business between stakeholders. For example, customer interaction with a business is buying products or services. Buying matches with commerce social interaction. Employees, suppliers and distributors can be matched with commerce, cooperation, collaboration, conflict, and coercion.

Can you think of ways communities are coerced? If you can't, you will read later about a water bottling factory.

BUSINESS AND SOCIETY TODAY

Market stakeholders of a business are:

1. Customers
2. Shareholders
3. Employees
4. Suppliers
5. Distributors
6. Creditors

Non-Market stakeholders of a business are:

1. Communities
2. Governments
3. Non-governmental organizations
4. Media
5. General public
6. Business support systems and groups

Whether you are an official citizen, like a market shareholder or stockholder of America, or an individual non-market American stakeholder, it benefits American society for your voice to be heard. This analogy can be used for any country, what you do matters, including whether you make your bed daily.

The purpose of the next chapter is to be aware of three ideas and how to act when your actions are needed to improve the quality of societies:

1. Bystander Effect
2. Whistle-blowing
3. Tacit Approval

Chapter 3: Relationship Management and Ethics

The relationship between market and non-market stakeholders can determine ethical stances. For example, if bottling water near a village in Nigeria earns a certain company profit, shareholders are content, but, at the expense of local villagers loss. After all, villagers are unable to afford the bottle water and then the river that supplies the village water begins to be contaminated by bottling factory pollution. Is it ethical for this business to be allowed to operate? How does it happen?

Governments allow businesses to operate factories whether leaders vote the approval for reasons of economic stimulus, bigger personal bank accounts, or whatever other reasons. If you had the chance to approve a factory to be built in your community that will offer jobs to community and first dibs on your family members to get those jobs, would you approve it?

Proxy voting was mentioned in Chapter 1. In the past, leaders have been fired from companies they have grown to be American household names. If you were ever left wondering how to prevent something like being fired from what you believe to be is your own company, then you need to know about controlling power.

If Steve Jobs held enough shares for majority votes or had proxy votes assigned to him to vote in his favor, enough to not be forced out of Apple, he could have prevented being forced out.

In more recent times, Elon Musk was forced to give up his seat as Chair of the Board of Directors of Tesla Inc., but still remain Chief Executive Officer. This was due to the fact that Tesla Inc. is a publically traded company and guidelines are to be abided to stay on good terms with regulators.

Let us move back to thinking on the government scale and how lobbyists influence lawmakers to vote or permit factories to be built in their communities. When it comes to relationships between government and business, proxy votes, as one can have within the corporate governance structure, do not exist. There may be no document or contract but indirect exchanges of favors or funds on verbal agreement, that voting for or against something can result in a deposit of funds in a bank account, does exist.

Attorney Generals have the job of investigating such acts. Meet Attorney General of New York, Letitia James, who filed a lawsuit against a gym in New York that continued to charge members and not honor cancellation requests through COVID-19 closures (Gross, 2020). Source: Forbes.

In conclusion, what we choose to do is for a benefit but whether that benefit is thought through, regarding later legal repercussions or health, we don't know.

When we are told stories from certain perspectives or given scenarios, we really do not know, for certain, how we would act in that scenario. We can get a feel by imagining, so imagine being in the scenarios that follow.

1. Your professor is speaking to you in person, one on one and has spinach in teeth. Do you say anything about it?
2. Your professor is presenting to a large audience and you are close to her and she has spinach in her teeth, do you tell her?

Watch the Bystander Effect video on EFTHEMIA YouTube Channel. Comments are enabled only for back end view, not public. Post a reply now.

By telling your professor about spinach in teeth you are not whistle blowing but doing something that has a similar energy to whistle blowing. Saying something by whistle blowing is tattling on co-workers, fellow-students, or bosses and leaders, when tattling must be done. My generation has the *snitches gets stitches* saying but deep down, there are many scenarios where saying something outweighs the repercussions of not.

Edward Snowden has been living in Russia because he is exiled from America for blowing the whistle on the National Security Agency (NSA) and Central Intelligence Agency (CIA). To learn more watch Snowden on Joe Rogan in 2019 and 2020 PowerfulJRE.

What would you do if you had a job being paid more than you needed to live and were stationed in a resort like area, not a stress in the world, except, while doing your job you noticed something not right, and looked deeper, and found evidence of unethical and maybe illegal behavior?

Unethical behavior can be legal, that is why this is quite an interesting area to learn more about. Since Edward Snowden came to the public eye, whistle blowers began to have protections. As for Snowden, $5.2 Million in profits from his book sales are to be relinquished to the United States government but it was found what he blew the whistle on can be deemed illegal. In summary, about the book, Snowden was allowed free speech and to publish what he wanted to publish but the court sided with the Department of Justice on perspective he breeched his contracts because prepublication review did not occur. I do not have an opinion regarding the Pardon Snowden petition. This lack of opinion leads to the discussion of tacit approval, but, if American voices vote to pardon Mr. Snowden, I would listen.

Imagine yourself in a group meeting for school, work, or any event. Depending on how comfortable you are in the group, you may say more or less. I had no issue correcting Grant Cardone regarding Benjamin Franklin in front of an entire audience in Anaheim, CA. I did not know anyone there but I could not stand by and let the audience be told Benjamin Franklin was a President of the United States, when he was not. If Mr. Cardone had spinach in his teeth, I am not sure what I would have done. Likely may have told one of his staff to tell him.

Now, imagine a meeting you actually sat in and someone said something that you did not agree with at all, but, you kept quiet, did not state your disapproval or speak up against a wrong statement. Not stating anything in response and keeping quiet, is tacit approval. It becomes implied that you approve of what was said or done, if you don't say something!

We have many social roles and in some we feel more comfortable speaking up than others. At work, we may fear retaliation, and that is a valid concern, hence, let unfair treatment or discrimination occur. As soon as we see from the perspective of others, and do it more often, we can increase our emotionally intelligence. If a coworker steps in to stop discrimination early, this can save a company in reputation later. Your actions matter because by letting unethical treatment occur in your workplace, a later scandal can lead to you losing your job because that workplace was sued and went bankrupt.

This next scene covers someone being bullied. If you were being bullied, would you want someone to step in and help you? By speaking up you can get the bully the help they need and the person being bullied out of a situation that could escalate.

Ethics are rooted in relationship management and the more perspectives you can see in business relationships and throughout, to all social roles you play, plus a dash of courage, the better any society you are a part of can become. Know your safety is important, but, if you can help someone to be safe, just do it.

Use the oxygen guideline:

BUSINESS AND SOCIETY TODAY

Chapter 4: Rights and Regulations

Businesses and governments are in a dance together in the United States of America, and in other parts of the world. It is because of the United States Constitution, that businesses are permitted to lobby and government can regulate businesses. These two *rights* dance and the leader of the dance can be either, at any time, to impact society.

Katie Porter asked a pharmaceutical company CEO why his salary is $120 Million USD and he answered because other pharmaceutical company CEO's make that much. Well why do they make that much in salary?

Lobbying to gain and maintain advantages with government related votes in favor for your products, drugs in this case, to pass, is needed, isn't it?

I can't say if these CEO's use their salary money for such reasons but having so much money puts them around people, places, and things that help them to continue to pursue their agenda's or goals. A goal can be to keep the businesses they lead highly profitable, even if it is at the expense of the health of people taking these drugs.

Fast tracking medication occurs. Fast tracking means a pharmaceutical company pays a higher fee and has minimum, but still legal, although, scientifically not robust, path to approve a drug or new medication for sale.

Legislation can also pass in favor of increasing the cost for drugs. Whether an insurance company or individual pays for drugs, the individual, in the end, pays for the insurance.

Multiply by many individuals addicted to the drugs or in need of drugs, it adds up. The citizens on Medicare who get the drugs, each pay for their prescriptions and then if the drug costs more, the government insurance, Medicare gets charged more, rendering a *Hippocritical* situation.

Hippocrates is known as The Father of Medicine and the term hypocritical can be described as a behavior of having a goal to keep people healthy but on the contrary make them unhealthy, dependent, and stressed. When the industry of healthcare sets aside health for wealth, why not call it Sickcare industry? Products that are offered to people by a for-profit organization can be categorized in the sickcare industry and non-profit organizations who operate ethically, keeping board member and management salaries regulated, are Healthcare.

Same argument about for-profit and non-profit goes for prisons that are privatized. Prisons have become almost the reverse of serving for the military, but, where a private company gets paid for having an inmate as opposed to a soldier being paid to serve in the military. A little about the military, for those who don't know, while serving in the military, your body is government property and so much as a sun burn can get you charged with destruction of government property.

I relate prison and military experience together because of how close they are to a coercive interaction. In a draft, young people can be forced to join the military and when someone is sentenced to prison, it is likely a place they really don't want to be.

Let us now get back to $100 Million USD in salary. With that much money, can someone avoid going to prison?

There are rights and regulations for all Americans to follow, and, human rights for all. America is great and being able to start businesses and become wealthy is fantastic but when do businesses need a wake-up call? Is it when the business supply chain is caught using child labor? Is it when the drug that a business sells has side effects that outweigh the benefit?

It is 2020 and in America, businesses with lobbying have been leading the dance for a while. Even when it comes to regulation, lobbyists can pay their way to ensure regulations don't impact their profits by using the profits they made to keep that cycle going.

What are some ideas that you have to give the power back to the people?

How can more political figures, who actually represent the people, serve the people?

Chapter 5: Technology

This chapter is going to introduce technology from a social media perspective, continue by posing questions, and then summarize impacts of technology in other fields.

The television (TV) and the Internet are powerful. Before TV there was radio and before radio there were people standing on boxes or stages talking to influence others. There is a modern phrase: **standing on your soapbox**.

A soapbox is a platform which one stands on to talk about something they are passionate about. The term comes from wooden crates being used for shipments of retail products from manufacturers, of which were dry goods or soap. People used these crates to be elevated and give their speech or express themselves.

There is a cognitive bias, **the soapbox effect**, where humans can trust the word of someone standing on a soapbox or stage, talking on the radio, TV, and Internet because of the elevated perspective. Today, almost everyone with access to the Internet has a sort of elevated platform, the Internet or the **micro platforms** to use and express themselves and digitally count their **reach**. A person standing on a soapbox had the reach of those in physical proximity to influence, the Internet allows for global influence.

What does reach matter? Reach today is what radios and TV had by broadcasting. Now, broadcasting uses the Internet. Internet micro platforms are websites, applications, and social media organizations. Users can pay for their content to reach more people using ads and pages can have compelling content to gain subscribers or followers. The micro platforms have algorithms though that can suggest who to follow or friend based on how a programmer wrote the code or the code has written itself for the purpose of obtaining active users and high engagement.

If we put all ways people can be influenced in a bucket called **media**, coverage is a way a more representative of the people public servant can serve the people. Serving the people, in the military, government, or organizations can take sacrifices. A celebrity that takes a stance regarding a social view they have can alienate fans, and, increase or decrease their likelihood of being cast or hired. The same goes for each individual based on the content they post online. Online can be forever and digital can be forever too. A picture stored to the cloud, no matter how private one thinks it is, is really not. Media accounts set to private still contain data on that platform. Once out there, content and data about a user can make their life better or worse. On a side note, the most cost effective way to get publicity is to be on the news. The power elite know this and perpetuate what they know the people will tune in to, hence, the nature of what is covered on the news. Fortunately, because of the Internet, people can choose what to tune into as long as they are aware of the cognitive bias called **confirmation bias**.

Watch Dr. Pop Cognitive Bias Confirmation on YouTube Channel EFTHEMIA

Technology impacts business and society in ways unimaginable at the time of inception. The generation of toddlers on mobile devices today, humanity won't know some impacts until twenty years later. If you were to hear a jingle or rhyme for an ad from childhood, it could get your attention. Rhymes that **go viral** can have a great impact on society. For example, "if it doesn't fit, you must acquit," is a rhyme from the 90's and the situation that rhyme stemmed from still has influence in society today by association.

Memes, advertising jingles, quotes from films, and the news at a time, impact a generation. I was in elementary school and one day we had the TV in our classroom to watch the launch of a space shuttle with astronauts in it and that space shuttle exploded. This undoubtedly impacted my generation, and the lack of funding for space programs perpetuated for a while, possible from the trauma of that event. Today, we as a species are making more traction in space exploration, but, the impact of what children saw, conscious or subconsciously, was a data point in their brain. The data in our brain influences our decisions.

Internet memes, jingles and sayings from influencers are now profoundly getting in the brains of people tuned in. What is consumed conscious or subconsciously can be controlled to a certain extent. The use of notifications and **click bait** can make the user of technology, not use, but, be used by technology. Today, it is challenging to find a great read on the Internet that is not infested with ads or other click bait, even on platforms we have accounts. My **aversion to ads** and commercials on the radio resulted in me making what were called mix tape recordings that cut the ads out. I stopped watching television very early, in high school. Occasionally, I will be somewhere and TV is playing. Today, watching streaming video has even turned me to repulsion with the previews of other shows to watch being advertised by video streaming service. Being connected ultimately means being connected to the social mainstream of what media broadcasts and to others.

August 10, 2020 in Crete, Greece
Video chat with masked non-bandit in CT

Technology opened up humans to connect with humans around the globe but technology is much more.

Ponder on advancements technology has impacted in these fields:

Medical

Medical devices, vaccines, and pharmaceuticals can be considered advanced technology in the field of medicine. We live in a time where some medical devices have not been tested long enough to know if they help the patient more than harm. We entrust our government to approve the use and distribution but when we know the power lobbying has, a degree of skepticism for what we put in to our body can arise.

There are populations of patients who say they don't trust pills and many who believe their life depends on them. It is up to the individual to decide but medical doctors are influencers. If a pharmaceutical company gives free samples and incentives to push a drug, do medical doctors do their bidding? Some do some don't. Be your own doctor first.

If a CEO from a pharmaceutical company has a salary of $120 Million USD a year, what does that mean for the lobbying budget? Even government regulations can be influenced at that point.

Production and Manufacturing

In the 1960's, it was the new thing to do to use pesticides and chemicals to yield more crops and produce more food. Today, we can have a **genetically modified organism (GMO)** be our food. Countries around the world have banned the use of GMOs but in the United States it is not banned. In recent times, the US had the most acres of GMO crops in the world.

Manufacturing factories are becoming more technology enhanced with the use of robots. Arguments today consist of machines and robots taking over human jobs. Typically, when a machine takes over doing a human job that human can pursue something with greater meaning.

Tractors and combine harvesters are machines that do the work my 96 year old grandmother did by hand when she was young. She also hand washed clothes when we spent our summers in Greece in the 80's. The washing machine made a task easier, as the dish washer also does today.

Yiaya Evlambia July 16, 2020

Energy

Today, fusion power is technologically challenging as was battery technology to store electricity, especially for the use of transport. Battery technology is improving the more attention we give it and although fusion powered electricity is challenging to harness, it requires more attention. As humanity had motivation to improve battery technology for optimal use of **solar** and wind energy, energy from fusion on earth is not a reality yet, because it needs more attention.

Solar powered structures harnessing energy from roof tops that were costly, have technologically advanced today to be a cost effective option. These roof tops work well with batter technology to store the energy so a power outage due to grid overload will not be a problem if the structure, home or commercial building, is **off the grid**.

Imagine how you can live off the grid?

Dr. P in front of Ecocapsule® at NYCxDESIGN Festival
Times Square May 18, 2019

Organizational Operations

An organizational operations overhaul of the decade just happened. Although technology to work from home has been around for over a decade, why did humans still go to the office or onsite, when in fact, it could have been more efficient for them to not? There are pro's and con's to working remotely and pro's and con's to delivering products or services online. There are some things we can learn online and some we need the hands on. Societies around the globe are now phasing to what extent organizations that comprise them will be like in terms of contact verse contactless interaction. What accelerated the use of more technological enhancement for organizational operations? **COVID-19**.

If leaders with controlling power have interests in not changing the business to operate more efficiently because change is challenging and a change could result in them not profiting in other areas, voters who don't care to know the complexities of matters, can permit proxy voting, and those in power and profiting stay in power. For example, property management companies in Southern California feed off the members who pay for the home owners association (HOA). If a management company has a contract to manage the HOA they can influence the board of directors on which landscapers, roofing companies, and types of services to use. Among making the association dependent on other services that could lead to conflict of interest.

One profit center for property management companies is charging the HOA fees to hard copy mail information and refusing to go lower cost paperless because then the profit from costs they charge to mail would not exist. It is a tiny bit complex to understand but not as complex as improving battery technology. Why the *tacit approval* for HOA dues?

People can just not want to learn or even try to know. Never fear the time it may take to understand something. If one truly cares about a matter, the focus on that matter, and repeated focus, results in deeper understanding. If a person states they love someone or something, focus on that person or thing can show love, and, result in better understanding. Be in the know.

The going contactless in 2020 has its pro's and con's. The new normal way of doing business and interacting in society has changed. Efficiency gains that organizations were force to adapt to, are challenging to implement. Once the gains are evident, like with washing clothes, why hand wash when we got used to the more efficient on human time way, using a washing machine?

Yes, tech gear and cyber security upgrades were needed but the benefits outweigh the cost. Take a stand for more remote work and school options where reasonable.

Wrap Up

In this short read we went on a journey to become familiar with business, government, and society field from perspective of Dr. P with her background in sociology, law, psychology, and statistics.

Post on Bystander Effect comments with word: QUESTION

Glossary

aversion to ads is a misos or hate, dislike, deep repulsion to advertisements, media using a compliance technique or psychology to trick a human to consume or buy a product or service.

click bait is an image, media, or a title that is interesting to human nature but actual material of media after clicking does not cover the material baited to click on an land, read, or become an active user statistic on the page click. Baited to click and add counts, views or active user data which subsequently can generate ad revenue.

confirmation bias is a human brain glitch that make humans stick to looking up, reading, referencing, researching or listening to beliefs they currently have and not constructively having an open mind for a different view.

COVID-19 stands for corona (CO) virus (VI) disease (D) in the year 2019.

electric car is a zero emissions fully electric powered automobile vehicle. It typically has a battery that requires charging. Note electricity generated from coal to charge such a car still not ideal but at least exhaust doesn't compound the pollution.

Federal government is an organization with powers given from the U.S. Constitution for the three branches of legislative, executive, and judicial, that comprise it, for governance.

Federal jurisdiction is the scope the federal government has in areas to handle legal issues.

genetically modified organism (GMO) is an organism of any including but not limited to plant, animal, and microorganism with engineered genome.

global means to impact around the globe of Earth and influence across borders and societies.

go viral means for a piece of content to get around in the media, especially on the Internet, to masses in a society or globally.

macro organization is a big group or team(s) of people working together or associated in society.

media audio and visual content that impacts society.

micro organization is a small group or team(s) of people working together or associated in society.

micro platforms are the small and nearly countless platforms on the Internet. If the entire Internet is the macro, the micro are all the websites and social media, smaller platforms that comprise it.

multi-national is to involve more than one country or society in business or with ideas.

off the grid is living without public utility electricity, water, and gas. It can extend to mean living without personal data about location, habits, and spending being documented or collected and stored.

organization is a group or team(s) of people working together or associated in society.

primary socialization is the first socialization or learned feelings an embryo, fetus, infant, and child receive regarding the values, appropriate feelings, and actions. A pregnant female under stress will result in the fetus feeling the stress, thus, socializing the fetus that having that stress is normal for them because that is what they learned.

proxy voting is signing over power of a voter to another so that other votes for them.

reach means how many views, clicks, landings, shares, likes or broadcast power that content or influencer has.

secondary socialization is the experiences that teach a person how to behave in micro groups within the macro of society like on a sports team, in class, at the office, in church, with supervising managers or abiding by guidelines to operate a business.

solar means of the sun.

stakeholder is an individual with interest or concern.

state constitution is each states own constitution.

streaming music is the combination of sounds using instrument or voice published or un-officially published as a file that is played over the Internet on or off demand.

the soapbox effect is a feeling to be on a higher platform to share a passionate message and being perceived as having a message worth value because on a platform.

Hyperlink References

California 2pac feat Dr.Dre – California Love HD
https://youtu.be/5wBTdfAkqGU

Confirmation bias Dr. Pop Cognitive Bias Confirmation
https://youtu.be/TIrhaKrkDxg

Entire audience in Anaheim, CA Αλɛi"th" ία από μένα -
Jan 11 2020 Ψεύτες https://youtu.be/1tdlxXe_BOI

Forbes N.Y. Attorney General Sues Sports Club

Freestyle music Diamond Girl
https://youtu.be/0Z3RYOeJhTM

Fun Hat Tricks ft. on Last Week Tonight with John Oliver
https://youtu.be/CyDdxktKxbU

Heart The Heart in the Robot
https://www.imdb.com/title/tt7083156/?ref_=nm_flmg_slf_
1

Open mind for a different view Metallica: Nothing Else
Matters (Official Music Video)
https://youtu.be/tAGnKpE4NCI

PowerfulJRE Joe Rogan Experience #1536 – Snowden
https://youtu.be/_Rl82OQDoOc

Story [NEW HERO – AVAILABLE] Orisa Origin Story |
Overwatch https://youtu.be/Lvm0of3iDUU

Made in the USA
Las Vegas, NV
17 September 2024